SUPER GEAR

Nanotechnology and Sports Team Up

Jennifer Swanson

Charlesbridge

To my dad, who gave me my love of sports, from his favorite daughter

Published by Charlesbridge
85 Main Street
Watertown, MA 02472
(617) 926-0329
www.charlesbridge.com

Library of Congress Cataloging-in-Publication Data
Swanson, Jennifer.
    Super gear: nanotechnology and sports team up/by Jennifer Swanson.
        pages cm
    ISBN 978-1-58089-720-4 (reinforced for library use)
    ISBN 978-1-60734-876-4 (ebook)
    ISBN 978-1-60734-877-1 (ebook pdf)
1. Sports—Technological innovations. 2. Sporting goods. 3. Performance technology. 4. Sports sciences.
I. Title.
GV745.S93 2016
688.7'6—dc23   2015017347

Printed in China
(hc) 10 9 8 7 6 5 4 3 2 1

Display type set in Nulshock by Typodermic and ITC Franklin Gothic
Text type set in Adobe Garamond Pro
Color separations by Colourscan Print Co Pte Ltd, Singapore
Printed by 1010 Printing International Limited in Huizhou, Guangdong, China
Production supervision by Brian G. Walker
Designed by Martha MacLeod Sikkema

Title page: A sprinter digs deep as he starts his race, not for a second thinking
of the nanotech equipment that may help him win.

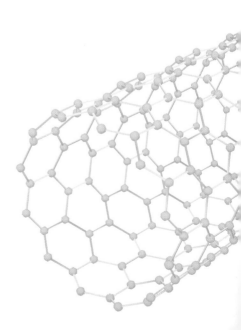

 # Table of Contents

Introduction

Olympic gold medalist Michael Phelps adjusts the hood of his parka and pulls it closer in an attempt to shut out the noise from the crowd. He knows the hardest part of swimming is the waiting. He goes over his swim in his mind, reviewing every stroke, every turn, and every breath. His attention is entirely focused on the swim ahead of him. The last thing he is worried about is his swimsuit. Michael knows that the special science used to create his suit will help him speed through the water.

Serena Williams rocks from side to side, reflexes on edge. The tennis ball hurtles toward her. *Whack!* She slams it back across the net and flips her racket around in her hand, ready for another volley. Serena is confident and focused. She doesn't even think about the science that was used to make her racket lighter, stronger, and more efficient.

Michelle Wie steps up to the tee. She cups her hand over her eyes and stares down the fairway, spying her target: a tiny spot on the grass more than two hundred yards away. Directing her thoughts to the golf ball in front of her, she adjusts her stance. She takes a deep breath, pulls the club back, and swings. *Crack!* The ball sails through the air, heading toward the hole. Confidently, Michelle leans over and plucks the tee from the ground. She strides toward her ball, not once thinking about the science used to create her club.

Track star Usain Bolt steps up to the starting blocks and fixes his gaze on the finish line at the end of the short, hundred-meter

Serena Williams relies on a racket enhanced with carbon nanofibers for a more powerful serve.

track. With the call of "on your mark," he stretches first one leg, then the other, and folds himself into the blocks. The spikes on his running shoes grip the specially designed racetrack. His muscles tense as he waits for the starting gun. *Bang!* He is off like a shot, sprinting down the track. Seemingly without much effort, he crosses the finish line, well ahead of his fellow runners. As he slows his pace after the race, Usain smiles to the crowd, totally indifferent to the technology in his shoes and the track that just helped him win.

What do Michael Phelps, Serena Williams, Michelle Wie, and Usain Bolt have in common? All their equipment was made using nanotechnology.

Nanotechnology is the science of things at the nanoscale. It deals with microscopic particles called nanoparticles. Most people measure items in terms of meters or feet. Nanotechnology engineers measure objects in nanometers. *Nano-* means "one-billionth," so a nanometer is one-billionth of a meter.

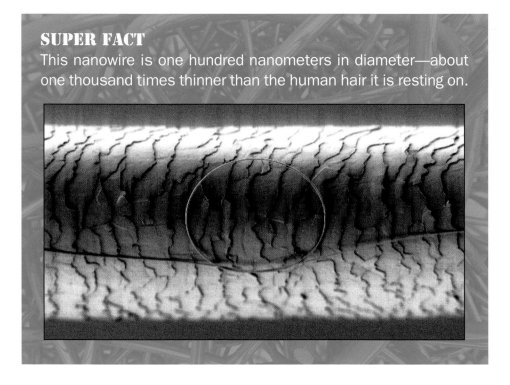

SUPER FACT
This nanowire is one hundred nanometers in diameter—about one thousand times thinner than the human hair it is resting on.

All That Glitters in Ancient Rome

The early Romans were the first to work with nanotechnology, although they didn't call it that. Archaeologists have discovered a cup from the fourth century CE that changes colors depending on the light. The color shift is caused by nanoparticles of gold and silver set into the glass. Although this may have been done by accident, it is evidence that humans have been aware of nanoparticles for quite some time.

A nanometer is so small, it is invisible to the human eye. Have you ever seen a single drop of water? The diameter of that water droplet is about 2.5 million times larger than a nanometer. Now look at the edge of this page. See how thin it is? A nanometer is one hundred thousand times smaller than that. Now that's tiny!

A nanoparticle is simply a teeny amount of a substance, up to one hundred nanometers in diameter. It is so small that you cannot see it without a special microscope.

Nanotechnology engineers work with nanoparticles to invent new materials with astonishing properties. In sports, nanotechnology is being used to create high-performance gear that is stronger, more durable, and capable of enhancing performance. Nanomaterials are found in many different kinds of sports equipment—from swimsuits to racing suits, from tennis rackets to golf clubs, from running shoes to racetracks, and pretty much everything in between. These microscopic marvels are part of a fast-moving, exciting new technology that is changing sports as we know it.

1

Tiny Bits of Science

Nanotechnology is the science of the very small

The science of nanotechnology starts at the smallest level of matter: the atom. Everything is made of atoms. Imagine the world as a bunch of microscopic building blocks where each block is one atom. Every chair, every desk, every *body* is made up of trillions upon trillions of blocks, or atoms, packed together. Even the air you breathe consists of atoms.

Of course you cannot see these atoms. An atom is approximately 0.1 nanometers in size. If you are about 4.5 feet (1.4 meters) tall, it would take almost 14 billion atoms stacked one on top of the other to equal your height. We're talking about some pretty small stuff!

Nanoparticles float through a carbon nanotube. (Artist's representation.)

It's rare to find atoms by themselves in nature; instead they tend to bond with other atoms. When two or more atoms bond together, they make a molecule. Oxygen, the second most common gas in the atmosphere, exists as a molecule, since it is formed when two atoms of oxygen bond together.

How the atoms are organized within a molecule plays an important part in what type of molecule is created and how that molecule functions. Take a water molecule, for instance. Water is made when two hydrogen atoms bond with an oxygen atom. As you probably know, water molecules at room temperature exist as a liquid, moving around fairly freely and bouncing off one another. When liquid water is cooled to the freezing point, though, the water molecules slow down and form a rigid crystalline structure, like a microscopic jungle gym. This arrangement of the water molecules leads to a change in the bonds between the atoms. Inside each water molecule, the hydrogen atoms shift slightly, moving just a little farther apart. That tiny change is enough to make a completely different type of substance: ice.

Water molecule

Liquid water

Ice

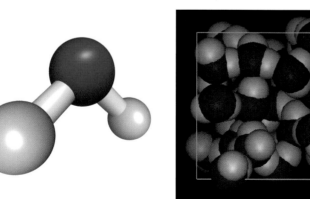
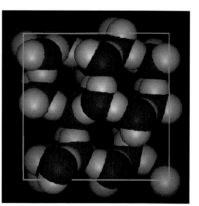

A molecule of water is made up of one oxygen atom (red) and two hydrogen atoms (white). Liquid water has a random arrangement of water molecules. Ice has a crystalline structure with each molecule in a specific place. (Artist's representation.)

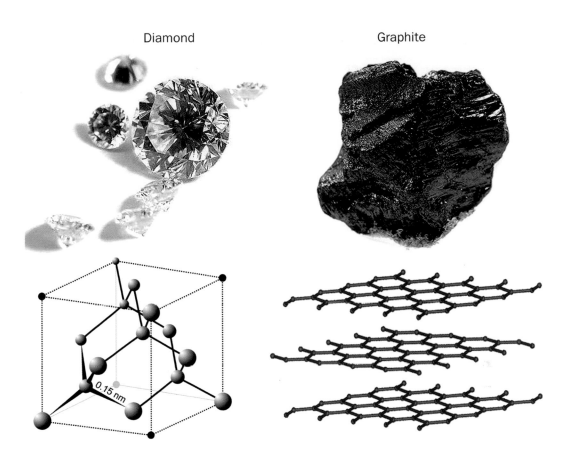

Diamond

Graphite

0.15 nm

Diamond and graphite are both made of carbon, but their molecular structures are completely different. (Artist's representation of molecules.)

Small changes in nanoparticles can have big effects on the substance

This same idea applies to the science of nanotechnology. A tiny change within a nanoparticle can lead to a completely different compound or material.

Graphite and diamond are both made of carbon, but they have very different properties. Carbon in the form of graphite, the substance found inside your pencil, is normally pretty soft. You can push on it without a lot of effort, and the graphite comes off on your paper. Carbon also occurs naturally as diamond, which is quite strong compared to graphite. Diamonds are so hard that they can be used to drill into other hard rocks. However, they are also brittle. With a sharp hit in the right place, they will crack and break.

The differences between graphite and diamond are a result of their molecular structure. In diamond, each carbon atom has a very strong bond with four other carbon atoms, which creates a tetrahedron, or four-sided crystal structure. It is very strong and hard to break. In graphite, each carbon atom bonds weakly with three other carbon atoms to form a sheet of carbon that looks like chicken wire. This produces a fairly soft substance.

But at the nanoscale, a sheet of graphite can be rolled into a tube, called a carbon nanotube. The three-dimensional arrangement of the tube creates a structure that is extremely strong—so strong that it is virtually indestructible. Carbon nanotubes are used to make golf clubs, tennis rackets, and baseball bats that pack a powerful punch.

Carbon Nanotube

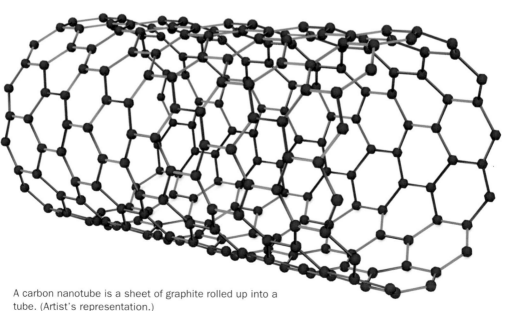

A carbon nanotube is a sheet of graphite rolled up into a tube. (Artist's representation.)

Nanoparticles are so tiny that they float around in the atmosphere with little regard to gravity. (Artist's representation.)

Tiny nanoparticles follow different rules of science

Why are carbon nanotubes so strong? It has to do with the size of the nanoparticle. Smaller particles fit more tightly together than larger particles, increasing the strength of the material. The atoms within a smaller particle also attract one another with greater force, resulting in stronger atom-to-atom bonds. The tighter bonds make for a much more durable substance. In a carbon nanotube the bonds between the carbon atoms are practically unbreakable.

The small size of a nanoparticle also means that gravity affects it less. To us, gravity is the most important force on Earth. It dominates everything we do. If you throw a ball, gravity makes it fall. If you jump up, gravity pulls you down. Gravity allows us to walk on the Earth without floating away. At the nanoscale, however, gravity functions a little differently. Gravity is directly related to mass, which means that nanoparticles, which have very little mass, are not affected much by it.

An example of this is the dust from a volcanic eruption. Volcanic dust includes nanoparticles of rock and dirt that stick together and are ejected into the air. These nanoparticles float around in the atmosphere until they are trapped by water molecules in a cloud. Within the cloud, the nanoparticles become attached to the much larger water molecules, which makes them bigger . . . and heavier. Now gravity becomes a greater factor, and the water (along with the dust particles) eventually falls to the ground as rain.

The microscopic size of a nanoparticle can even affect the color of the material. Smaller particles reflect light differently, which can result in our eyes perceiving a different color. While regular-sized particles of gold appear yellow in color, nanoparticles of gold, which are infinitely smaller, appear red or purple.

Particles at the nanoscale don't follow the same rules of science that the rest of us do. They form very tight bonds, which can make them stronger than steel, and yet they are so tiny, gravity doesn't have much effect on them. It's all due to their incredibly small size, which leads to unique characteristics.

Tiny nanoparticles have big surface area

Bond strength, color, and size aren't the only properties that change at the nanoscale. Working at the nanoscale allows engineers to play with surface area, the space that covers the outside of an object. Surface area can be increased by dividing something into smaller parts. Let's look at a potato, for instance. The entire outside of the potato is the surface area. But inside the potato are atoms that are not exposed to the surface. They don't count toward the total surface area.

Cut the potato in half. The surface area increases. Now cut the halves into french fries. The surface area of the potato increases more than tenfold. The same thing happens in nanotechnology.

A whole potato has less surface area than the same potato cut into slices or french fries, because more of it is underneath the surface.

A nanomaterial can be made up of billions and billions of nanoparticles. The outside of each nanoparticle counts toward the total surface area. This gives the nanomaterial a much greater surface area than that of a normal substance. The larger surface area allows for more interaction between particles. Now instead of just two larger particles interacting with each other, you may have ten nanoparticles sticking together. The extra interactions can speed up a reaction or improve the strength and durability of a product.

Try this experiment to see how surface area affects the behavior of a substance.

Materials:

2 glass cups

2 cups (470 milliliters) of very hot water

3 cups (600 grams) of granulated sugar

3 cups (380 grams) of powdered sugar (confectioners' sugar)

2 pieces of thin cotton string (about double the cup's height in length)

2 paper plates

2 pencils or wooden sticks

2 washers or other weights

Procedure:

1. Label one cup "granulated sugar" and one cup "powdered sugar."
2. Pour 1 cup (235 milliliters) of very hot water into each cup.
3. Pour the granulated sugar into one cup and the powdered sugar into the other cup. Stir until the sugar has dissolved. Note how long it took for each type of sugar to dissolve.
4. Put one string in each cup. Allow the strings to soak for about 5 minutes. Take them out and place them on separate paper plates.
5. Allow the strings to dry for about 10 minutes. Then take each string and tie one end to the middle of a pencil. Tie a washer to the other end.
6. Place each pencil across the top of a cup, so the string and washer hang down into the sugar solution.
7. Leave the strings in the solution for 4 to 7 days. Watch as crystals form on the strings. Then take the crystals out and look at them with a microscope or magnifying glass.

Ask Yourself:

Which sugar had more surface area? Did that sugar dissolve faster? Why? How are the crystals grown from the two types of sugar different?

So nanoparticles are different from regular particles in many ways:

- A tiny shift at the nanoscale can have a huge effect on the overall material.
- The smaller size of nanoparticles allows them to fit together more tightly.
- The greater forces of attraction within them make them stronger.
- Gravity has relatively little effect on them.
- They have more surface area, which can result in more interactions between particles.

Scientists and engineers take advantage of these unique properties to create amazing materials at the nanoscale—materials that we use in our everyday lives.

Nanotechnology is engineering on a small scale

What if you had the power to move atoms within a molecule? Or to move molecules and change how they bond to one another? You could make whatever you wanted. Imagine making a baseball bat one thousand times stronger than normal, without increasing the weight. The baseball would fly farther and faster with the same strong swing. Imagine being able to weave a piece of cloth so tightly together that it fits like a second skin. The smooth fit of the fabric would allow a swimmer to cut through the water more easily, increasing his or her speed. Sounds great, doesn't it?

All of this is possible through nanotechnology. By putting atoms together in different ways, engineers can make new nanoparticles. By moving nanoparticles around, they can create new nanomaterials.

Traditional manufacturers typically make products "from the top down." They take a piece of material and remove pieces of it until they have the size and shape they want. Think of making a

Traditional manufacturers create a shirt from the top down, cutting out the parts of the shirt from a larger piece of cloth.

shirt from a bolt of fabric. The parts of the shirt are cut out of one big piece of fabric. Then the unused scraps are thrown away.

What if you could make the same shirt starting at the molecular level? Each nanoparticle would be put in a specific place within the material. Nanoparticles would attach tightly to one another. More of them would be added until they finally formed a shirt. This is called engineering a product "from the bottom up," and it results in a stronger material that is more resistant to wear and tear. An added benefit is less waste and pollution. Since the shirt was created from individual nanoparticles, no scraps are left over.

Nanotechnology is changing the way we make all kinds of products, from sunscreen to biosensors to sports equipment.

Nanomanufacturers create products from the bottom up, moving nanoparticles around to make new materials. (Artist's representation.)

Nanoparticles can be moved around to create new materials

But how do you see nanoparticles—not to mention work with them? Nanoparticles are so small that they can't be seen with a normal microscope. Instead, nanotech engineers might use a special high-powered tool called a scanning tunneling microscope (STM). Unlike a normal microscope, which uses light to illuminate objects, an STM uses a tiny metal probe to scan nanoparticles. Electricity is applied to the probe, which is then moved across the nanoparticle. As the probe moves, it detects the tiny ridges and crevices of the nanoparticle. It uses that information to create a three-dimensional

STM Graffiti

Scanning tunneling microscopes can be used to create the tiniest graffiti in the world. Scientists at the Center for NanoScience (CeNS) in Munich, Germany, used an STM to print the name of their team on a graphite surface. The lines of each letter are about one to three nanometers wide. This graffiti is too small to be seen by the human eye, so the scientists probably won't get in trouble!

image. The probe can also be used to pick up and move individual atoms or nanoparticles. That sounds like a lot of work, doesn't it?

Engineers thought so. So they developed a new type of machine to make it easier to manipulate nanoparticles. Called an optical nanotweezer, this device moves nanoparticles with a tiny laser beam. Some optical nanotweezers are equipped with different options, including a gripper that allows the operator to grab and shift nanoparticles with the simple maneuver of a joystick.

But making a nanomaterial at the molecular level is time-consuming—even with the help of an optical nanotweezer. People can't make thousands of pieces of sports equipment bit by bit.

Matthias Bode uses a scanning tunneling microscope to observe individual atoms at the Center for Nanoscale Materials in Argonne, Illinois.

Instead, after a nanotech material is developed, sports companies figure out how to make a lot of it, fast. Some companies spray special nanocoatings on their gear. Others add nanopowders to their equipment or even weave special nanofibers into their materials. This is called nanomanufacturing.

Nanomanufacturing leads to sports equipment that is stronger, lighter, and more durable. Some nanotech gear is water-repellent, and some can even keep away smell or clean themselves. Sound unbelievable? It's not. Nanotechnology is involved in almost every piece of sports equipment made today. Not bad for a microscopic science that no one can see.

2
Super Suits

Nanotechnology is creating athletic "super suits"

Time. The *tick, tick, tick* of the clock affects almost every athletic event. From swimming to biking to running, the fastest person to finish is the winner. Athletes train for many hours every day to get their bodies to peak performance. They have one goal in mind: winning. Athletes compete not only against one another, but also against the forces of nature.

One force that affects everything an athlete does is drag. Drag is a force that slows a solid object down as it moves through a fluid. The fluid can be air or water. When you walk in a pool, you experience drag; it feels like the water is pushing back on you. Athletes need to be concerned with drag because it slows them down. For example, when you ride your bicycle on a windy day, you go more slowly because the wind is pushing back on you.

Michael Phelps dives off the starting block in his nanotech supersuit.

15

A streamlined, horizontal position helps a swimmer reduce drag and increase speed.

Swimmers have always known about drag, because they encounter it every time they step into the pool. Let's face it: while our skin is an amazing material that can stretch, breathe, and repair itself, it was never designed for speed swimming.

Ever taken a really long bath, gone swimming for an hour, or

Size and Drag

The size of an object affects how much drag there is on it. Imagine pushing a basketball through the water. You have to push pretty hard to get it to go forward. The force you provide pushes the water out of the way. But water is heavy, so it pushes back on the basketball, causing you to feel drag. Now imagine pushing a baseball through the water. It requires less force because the baseball is smaller. Because it has less surface area, less water needs to be moved out of the way and you feel less drag.

Want to see exactly how drag affects a swimmer in the water? Give this experiment a try.

Materials:
Plastic plate
Basketball
Baseball
The wing from a toy plane, or a big curved spoon (The object must have a curve to it like an airplane wing.)

Procedure:
1. Fill up your bathtub halfway with water.
2. Starting from one end of the tub, push each object through the water. Push the objects in a straight line and at the same approximate speed. How hard do you have to push on each object?
3. Look at each object as you push it. Does the water in front of the object ripple? How about behind the object?

Ask Yourself:
Which object was the most difficult to push through the water? Which object experienced the most drag?

just washed a lot of dishes? What happened to your hands? They probably started to wrinkle. The wrinkles happen partly because your skin isn't truly water-repellent. Once the natural oil covering your skin washes off, the outer layer of skin begins to soak up the water like a sponge. Absorbing the water makes your skin swell slightly, which increases its surface area. This increases drag.

And what about all that hair on your arms and legs, let alone your head? That slows you down, too. Each individual hair causes a tiny bit of drag on your body.

Speed skater Shani Davis crouches to decrease the effect of the drag from the air.

So what do competitive swimmers do about the drag problem? They wear suits that cover as much skin as possible. They also wear swim caps—or shave off their body hair before a meet. Believe it or not, it helps!

Swimmers can also reduce drag by keeping their bodies as horizontal as possible when swimming. When you stand upright and walk through the water, it takes a lot of energy because you are pushing lots of water in front of you. But if you are horizontal, with your head, shoulders, hips, and legs all on the same level, you are pushing less water and using less energy. You can cut through the water more easily.

Swimmers aren't the only ones who have to worry about drag. Runners and speed skaters are affected by drag as they move through the air. The stronger the drag, the slower they go. Ever wonder why a speed skater bends forward in a crouch while he races? It's to reduce the airflow over his body. A runner bends slightly forward during her run to allow the air to flow more smoothly over her partially hunched shoulders. While these practices help improve performance, it wasn't until nanotechnology was applied to the problem that drag was significantly reduced.

Nanotech suits decrease drag from the wind

Nanotechnology engineers are helping sports companies create specially designed athletic suits. These "super suits" are not just uniforms; they are also tools that improve an athlete's performance. They are helping athletes to get back the thing they want most: time.

Under Armour engineers tackled the problem of drag in speed skating by asking Lockheed Martin, a company that produces airplanes, for help. Drag slows down an airplane in the same way it

Drag on an Airplane

All airplanes are affected by drag, which is the force that pulls back on the plane as it flies through the air. Drag acts directly opposite to forward motion and is the main reason the plane requires energy to move forward. Drag works in the same way on a swimmer or speed skater.

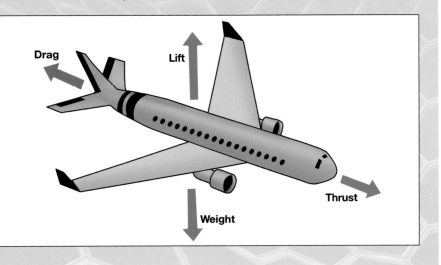

slows down an athlete. The Under Armour scientists figured that if they could see how Lockheed Martin reduced the drag on an airplane, they could use the same ideas for their new super suits.

It might seem that making the surface of a suit as flat and streamlined as possible would decrease drag. That's actually not true. When air flows over a smooth object at a fast speed, swirls of wind, or turbulence, occur behind the object. The turbulence slows it down. An athlete experiencing turbulence feels like he is pulling a weight behind him.

To decrease both turbulence and drag, Under Armour created a suit, called the Mach 39, with raised bumps across certain sections. The bumps molded the flow of air as it moved across the suit. By breaking up the air and funneling it in a specific direction, the bumps changed the pattern of the airflow behind the athlete. This reduced turbulence and, in turn, the overall drag on the athlete.

The key to creating the bumps was nanotechnology. Nanotechnology made it possible for five different materials to be seamlessly merged into a light, stretchy, and breathable fabric. On the outside of the fabric, nanoparticles of polyurethane were clumped together to form the tiny bumps. The bumps were placed on the hood, forearms, and lower legs—the places of greatest drag and friction—to enhance performance.

Under Armour and Lockheed Martin spent more than two years and three hundred hours testing their speed-skating suits on mannequins in a wind tunnel. The goal was to get the airflow just right—to create a suit that would be as aerodynamic as a fighter jet.

Nike has done similar tests with its full-body Pro TurboSpeed tracksuits, which also feature bumps made with nanotechnology. After spending more than one thousand hours testing their suits in a wind tunnel, engineers believe they have shaved 0.023 seconds off a hundred-meter run. While that reduction in time may seem small, in a short race like the hundred-meter, it can be the difference between first and third place.

Nanotech suits decrease drag from the water

The first nano-designed uniforms to make a big splash in the swimming world were the Speedo LZR Racer suits. Speedo developed these suits along with NASA, the National Aeronautics and Space Administration. It was a bit unusual for NASA to work with a swimsuit company. After all, NASA is a government organization that focuses on putting vehicles into space. But as Speedo's Stuart Isaac put it, "People would look at us and say, 'This isn't rocket science,' and we began to think, 'Well, actually, maybe it is.'"

The partnership with NASA turned out to be perfect. NASA knows a lot about drag, since drag has a huge effect on every rocket it sends into space. NASA also has wind tunnels, which are a great way to test the drag on a swimsuit. Air flowing across a suit in a wind tunnel is similar to water flowing across a swimmer in a pool.

Speedo engineers had determined that 25 percent of the total drag acting on a swimmer's body is caused by the water flowing across it. In an effort to reduce that effect, they asked NASA to test different fabrics in its wind tunnels.

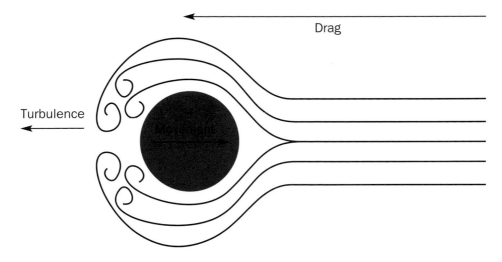

As an object pushes through water, the forces of drag and turbulence slow it down.

Based on the results, Speedo's Aqualab created the LZR suit out of tiny fibers of nylon and spandex woven very tightly together. The chest and backside of the suit were covered with thousands of microscopic ridges.

The special ridges were deemed groundbreaking. Like the bumps

Jamaican swimmer Alia Atkinson pushes through the water, applying great effort to overcome drag and turbulence.

Swimmers dive off the blocks, sporting the latest in compression-swimsuit technology.

on speed-skating and tracksuits, they were supposed to reduce drag. Unfortunately, that didn't happen. The ridges had little effect on drag reduction.

Still, the LZR suit was fast. As it turns out, its speed was due not to the ridges, but to the supertight fabric weave. Through nano-technology, the tiny fibers of nylon and spandex were woven so tightly that the fabric created a compression effect on the swimmer's body. This enhanced blood flow and increased muscle performance.

Custom-Fit Compression

Some swimwear companies create a three-dimensional image (avatar) of a swimmer. Computer simulations show engineers where the swimmer will experience the most drag and turbulence. Then an individually specific suit is created to compress those parts. The result? A swimsuit that makes the swimmer's body more tubelike and streamlined. The drawback? It's hard to put on! It can take a female swimmer up to nine different steps and more than thirty minutes to put on a compression swimsuit.

It also gave the swimmer's body a more streamlined, torpedo-like shape, similar to a shark's. This allowed the swimmer to glide through the water with less resistance.

The LZR suits were so fast, in fact, that more than 90 percent of swimmers who won medals at the 2008 Beijing Olympics were wearing them. The swimming world was stunned.

Today companies such as Speedo, Aqua Sphere, and Dolfin continue to improve on compression technology. Using nano-enhanced techniques, they have created swimsuits that stretch vertically, giving the swimmer freedom of movement, but not horizontally, keeping the body more streamlined.

Other swimwear companies are using nanofibers to create special bands in the fabric of their swimsuits. These bands provide support but also stretch with the swimmer as he or she moves.

Nanocoatings are making swimsuits waterproof and buoyant

Most traditional swimsuits are not completely waterproof. Instead, the fabric absorbs some of the water and becomes wet, slowing

Water beads up and rolls off the nanocoating of a waterproof fabric.

Without nanofilaments

Water

Fabric

© Hohenstein Institute

With nanofilaments

Water

Air cushion of microbubbles

Nanofilaments

Fabric

A coating of nanofilaments can make a swimsuit waterproof and more buoyant. The nanofilaments attract microbubbles, creating a cushion of air between the swimsuit fabric and the water. The air keeps the fabric from getting wet—and helps the swimmer to float. Water also flows more smoothly over the cushion of air, decreasing turbulence and drag.

the swimmer down. But the new nanotech super suits are almost completely waterproof. As the swimmer cuts through the water, the water rolls off the fabric. Like the skin of a shark, the fabric does not absorb water. The result is a faster, sleeker swimmer with a super-speedy racing time.

The trick to making the suits waterproof is applying a thin layer of silicon nanofilaments to the fabric. These nanofilaments have microscopic spikes that keep the water from being absorbed. Water droplets sit on top of the spikes and can't get to the fabric. The nanofilaments are like guardians that don't allow the water to pass. The coating is permanently attached and makes the fabric

Super Suits for Everyone

Nanotech swimsuits aren't just for athletes. New recreational swimsuits with nanofibers are water- and stain-repellent. They come in all sizes and colors, and hold up in salt water, chlorine, and multiple washes in the washing machine. The suits are designed for men, women, and children, and can even come with matching nanotech goggles and caps. The goggles have a special nanocoating that prevents them from fogging up in the water.

Missy Franklin gets off to a great start in her nanotech suit.

extremely water-repellent. The super suit stays dry, even if it's kept underwater for long periods of time.

Another advantage of the nanofilaments is that they trap a layer of air between the water and the fabric. The air makes the swimmer more buoyant. The swimmer's body is better supported by the water and thus can move faster through it.

The waterproof, buoyant super suit, with its compression technology, reduces drag from the water by almost 20 percent. That makes the swimmer's time much, much faster.

Whether you are climbing on a starting block by a pool or digging your toe into the ice before a race, every second counts. On your mark, get set, go!

3

Super Bats, Rackets, and Clubs

Carbon nanotubes make baseball bats stronger and lighter

Crack! A baseball bat connects with a ball. The ball sails over the fence. Home run! The crowd goes wild! Most spectators don't really think about the forces involved in hitting a ball. But did you know that some of the energy from the swing is actually transferred to the ball when it's hit? In general, the faster the swing, the harder the impact on the ball, and the farther the ball flies.

So what type of bat is best: wood or aluminum? Baseball fans have been arguing this question for decades. The answer comes down to three things: the weight of the bat, the point of impact, and how the material bounces back when it's hit.

The weight of the bat determines the speed of your swing. You want a bat that is light enough to swing easily but heavy enough to pack a powerful punch. Aluminum bats are hollow inside, so

Albert Pujols steps up to the plate, ready to hit the ball out of the park.

29

A Stinging Reminder

Have you ever swung a bat? When you connect with the ball, sometimes vibrations travel down the bat and make your hand sting a little. That means you didn't hit the ball with the sweet spot. If the ball hits the sweet spot, you will feel fewer vibrations because the majority of the energy goes into the ball.

you might think they are lighter than wooden bats, but that's not always the case.

The point of impact, or the place where the bat hits the ball, also has a lot to do with how far the ball flies. As all batters know, the best point of impact is called the sweet spot. The sweet spot is the point where the maximum amount of the batter's energy is transferred to the ball, sending it higher and farther. When you are picking your bat, you want one with a wide sweet spot. Typically, aluminum bats have a larger sweet spot, which means you are more likely to hit the ball with that part of the bat.

Finally, the elasticity of the bat also plays a role in the distance the ball travels. A wooden bat is solid throughout, so it is not flexible; it lacks elasticity. When it connects with the ball, the bat absorbs some of the ball's energy. The ball slows down slightly, requiring the batter to provide more power to send it flying into the outfield. An aluminum bat, on the other hand, is hollow and bounces back like a trampoline. Rather than absorbing the energy from the ball, the bat reflects the energy back into the ball. The ball keeps most of its original energy, as well as the energy from the swing.

From a scientific point of view, aluminum seems like it should be the clear winner in the great bat debate: aluminum bats can be lighter than wooden bats, and they have a bigger sweet spot and greater elasticity. But new nanocomposite bats are making the choice more complicated.

Want to find the sweet spot of your baseball bat? Get a friend and try this experiment.

Materials:
Baseball bat
Hammer

Procedure:
1. Hold the bat in one hand so that the barrel hangs down toward the ground.
2. Have your friend tap lightly on the bat with the hammer, starting at the bottom of the bat. As the bat is struck, you should feel your fingers tingling.
3. Have your friend slowly move up the bat, tapping as he or she goes. When the tapping does not cause a tingling sensation in your fingers, you've found the sweet spot of the bat.

Ask Yourself:
Why is the sweet spot the best place to hit the ball? Is it just because that's the part that makes your fingers tingle less? Try this experiment with different types of bats to see how weight, length, and material affect the location of the sweet spot.

A traditional composite bat consists of carbon fibers fused together with resin. In 2005 the Easton Bat company took the composite bat one step further. The Stealth CNT bat, the world's first nano-composite bat, integrated carbon nanotubes.

What Is Resin?
Resin is a thick, sticky substance that is used as a filler to provide strength in many products. Tree sap is a type of natural resin. Companies use synthetic resin in composite baseball bats to give them strength, durability, and better shock absorbance.

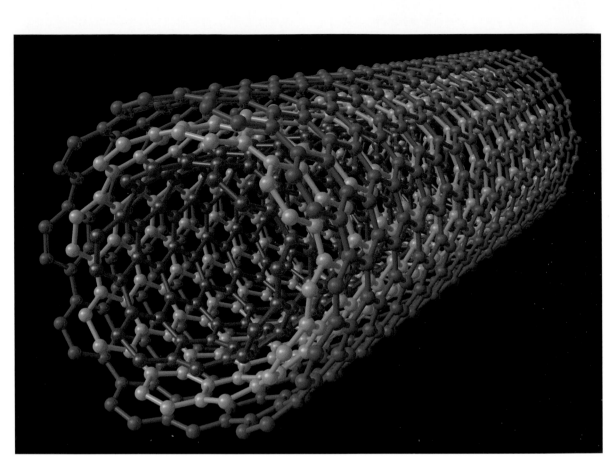

Multiwalled carbon nanotubes (carbon nanotubes placed one inside the other) are added to baseball bats to give them extra strength. (Artist's representation.)

To make a carbon nanotube, chains of carbon atoms are arranged in hexagon shapes. These repeating hexagons form a single sheet that is rolled into a tube. A carbon nanotube can be one-billionth of a meter wide and sixteen times stronger than steel. The nanotubes are small enough to be placed between the carbon fibers of a composite bat. This gives the bat extra strength, without adding much weight.

A nanocomposite bat is lighter than an aluminum bat, which makes it easier to swing. It has a large sweet spot like an aluminum bat. The carbon nanotubes also increase the bat's elasticity. The result is a bat that can make the ball fly faster and farther, which makes it much easier to get a home run.

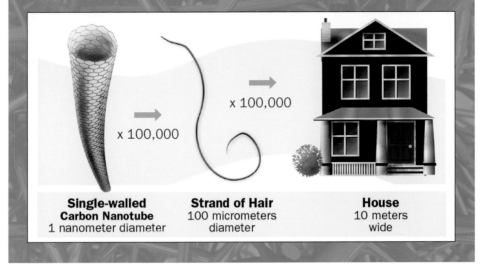

| Single-walled Carbon Nanotube 1 nanometer diameter | Strand of Hair 100 micrometers diameter | House 10 meters wide |

In fact, nanotech bats—and aluminum ones, too—are so effective that Major League Baseball (MLB) does not allow its professional players to use them. They must use wooden bats instead. Nanotech bats are, however, allowed in Little League, high school, and some college games. So next time it's your turn to choose a bat, pick one that will hit it out of the park. Batter up!

No Nanotech Bats for Pros

So why don't professional baseball players use aluminum or nanotech bats? One reason is that they are considered to be too dangerous. The speed of the ball coming off an aluminum bat can be up to 20 miles (32 kilometers) per hour faster than a ball hit with a wooden bat. That's pretty fast when you consider that many MLB pitchers throw pitches at speeds greater than 90 miles (145 kilometers) per hour. The other reason is that MLB wants to keep the sport focused on the skill and athletic ability of the individual player, not on the technology-enhanced tools that he is using.

Novak Djokovic returns the ball with his graphene racket.

Graphene is taking tennis rackets to a new level

Baseball is not the only sport with carbon nanotubes in its equipment. Tennis rackets have them in their strings. The carbon nanotubes make the strings stronger and less likely to break than traditional natural-gut or synthetic strings. The nanotubes are also more elastic, springing back like a trampoline when the ball hits them. The energy from the athlete's swing is transferred more efficiently to the ball, and the ball bounces back harder. *Thwap!* A stronger, more powerful return.

In 2002 the French company Babolat introduced the first tennis-racket frames enhanced with carbon nanotubes. Babolat claimed that these frames were one hundred times stronger than steel but one-sixth the weight. The nanotubes were also much stiffer than the graphite in traditional rackets, which made the nanotech racket easier to control. The VS Nanotube Power racket packed a powerful punch! Tennis players flocked to the new technology.

But nanotechnology is always changing. Today carbon nano-tubes in the frames of tennis rackets are being replaced with a new nanomaterial called graphene. Graphene is considered the strongest material in the world. As one scientist puts it, "It would take an elephant, balanced on a pencil, to break through a sheet of graphene the thickness of Saran Wrap."

Tennis rackets containing graphene tend to be larger than normal rackets, which makes it easier to hit the ball. But they are still lightweight.

Because graphene is so strong, tennis manufacturers have also been able to change the weight distribution of their rackets. In a traditional graphite racket, the handle is relatively heavy compared to the head (the oval part). But when the graphite in the handle is

Great Graphene

Graphene is a carbon nanotube laid flat: a single sheet of carbon atoms bonded together like a chain-link fence. Impossible as it may seem, unrolling a carbon nanotube changes it into a new nanomaterial with unique properties. A graphene nanoparticle is smaller and stronger than a carbon nanotube. Its tiny size makes it a great fit between other atoms. Adding graphene flakes to other materials makes the end products extremely strong and durable.

Super Bats, Rackets, and Clubs   35

Graphene is one of the strongest materials on the planet, but it is so thin and flexible you can bend it with your fingers. (Artist's representation of molecular structure.)

replaced with graphene, the handle becomes much lighter. The weight shifts to the head and grip, making for a smoother, more powerful swing.

The combination of all of these qualities allows for a more powerful swing. Novak Djokovic, a world-class tennis player, has won multiple tournaments with his graphene racket.

Bouncy Is Better

When a tennis ball is made, compressed air is trapped inside. Every time the ball bounces, a little bit of air leaks out. Eventually, the ball loses its bounce. Tennis companies, such as Wilson, have developed a nanocoating that allows tennis balls to hold their bounce longer. Tiny, closely packed nanoparticles form a barrier that traps the air more effectively. The ball stays bouncy twice as long as a regular tennis ball. A bouncy ball absorbs the energy from the racket better, making for a more powerful return.

Michelle Wie tees off with a powerful swing of her nanotech golf club.

Nanotechnology gives golf clubs durability and strength

Professional golfers such as Phil Mickelson and Michelle Wie look for the latest technology when choosing a club. Their highly specialized golf clubs incorporate nanotechnology to improve the accuracy of their swings and increase the distance of their drives.

A golf club has three main parts: (1) the grip, where the golfer holds the club, (2) the shaft, the long part of the club, and (3) the head, the part of the club that hits the ball. Nanotechnology is being used to improve all three parts.

The grip is made of strong elastomers, or elastic polymers, that are soft yet firm to the touch. When the ball connects with the head of the club, vibrations travel up the shaft to the grip. The

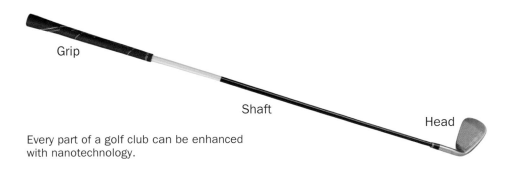

Grip

Shaft

Head

Every part of a golf club can be enhanced with nanotechnology.

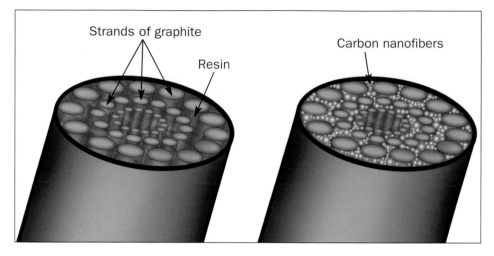

In the newest golf clubs, nanofibers are added to the resin of the shaft to close up the gaps between the strands of graphite.

elastomers in the grip help absorb the energy of the vibrations, keeping the golfer's hands from stinging. The grip can be sprayed with a special nanocoating that keeps it soft, shiny, and dirt-free.

In a typical composite golf club, the shaft is composed of long strands of graphite (similar to the graphite in your pencil) encased in resin. In some nanotech clubs, carbon nanofibers are added to the resin, filling the space between the long graphite strands. The stiff nanofibers make the shaft stronger. They also help dampen some—but not all—of the vibrations from the club striking the ball. This helps the player gauge the strength of his or her swing without losing stability.

Soft at Heart

Some golf companies, such as Nike and Bridgestone, are creating nanotech balls that have an inner core made of water or thermoplastic resin, a plastic that can be heated, molded, and cooled. The idea behind this technology is that the ball will have both a hard outside *and* a soft core. Golfers want hard balls that fly farther down the fairway, but softer balls that are easier to hit when putting on the green. The new balls do both.

Phil Mickelson swings for longer distance with his technology-enhanced golf club.

The weakest part of the golf club is where the tip of the shaft is attached to the head. The tip is strengthened by placing carbon nanotubes between layers of titanium. A stronger tip gives the player more control when he or she pulls the club back to swing.

The head of the golf club incorporates nanotechnology in the face, where the golf ball is struck. Inside the titanium face, there is a plate of high-density carbon nanocomposite, which provides support and stiffness for harder, more controlled impact with the ball.

To understand how a stronger golf club affects a player's game, let's break down a golf swing. When you swing the club, you are applying force to the ball through your arms and the club. A strong shaft transfers that force directly to the club face, which in turn transfers it to the ball. The *chink* you hear when you strike the ball means a lot of energy has gone into the ball. It travels higher and farther down the fairway. Fore!

4

Super Shoes

Nanotechnology makes shoes stronger and more durable

Speed. It's what every runner wants. Run faster and you win the race—at least that's the idea. Athletes train hard for their events. Sprinter Usain Bolt works out daily to stay in top shape. He hops, he jumps, he bounds, all to keep his muscles strong. He practices his starts until they are lightning quick. He lifts weights and does trial runs of his events, the hundred-meter and two-hundred-meter dashes. His ultimate goal is to stay at the top of his sport for as long as possible.

What else can he do? Buy the right shoes. While keeping fit is a huge part of being an athlete, the other part is picking the right equipment. For a runner, that means a good shoe—one that provides

The right shoes are the most important gear for a runner.

41

support, protection, and comfort. Nanopolymers are being used to create amazing new running shoes that provide all of that, plus durability, which makes them last for a long time.

Nanopolymers help absorb energy in running shoes

Running shoes are made to absorb energy. As your foot hits the pavement, it transfers energy to the ground. Since the ground is hard, most of the energy is reflected back to your foot. Have you ever run barefoot on a sidewalk or road? After a while your feet

Outsole

Insole

Midsole

The bottom of a shoe is made of three parts: the outsole, the midsole, and the insole. All three can be enhanced with nanotechnology.

start to hurt because they are absorbing all that reflected energy. When you wear running shoes, the materials in the shoes absorb the energy. To do that, the shoes must be soft and kind of squishy. But if you ran on soft and squishy shoes all the time, they would eventually flatten out. Then you would feel the road under your feet again and they would hurt. The solution? Foam.

Foam is great at absorbing energy, but it also provides the support you need. The midsoles of traditional running shoes are made of a flexible, rubberlike foam called ethylene vinyl acetate, or EVA. EVA foam is made of polymers, or long chains of molecules strung together. Pockets of gas are trapped between the polymers. When the shoe hits the pavement, the polymers are compressed, causing them to release a tiny amount of additional gas into the space between them. The gas makes the polymers rebound, or bounce back, absorbing the energy of the impact.

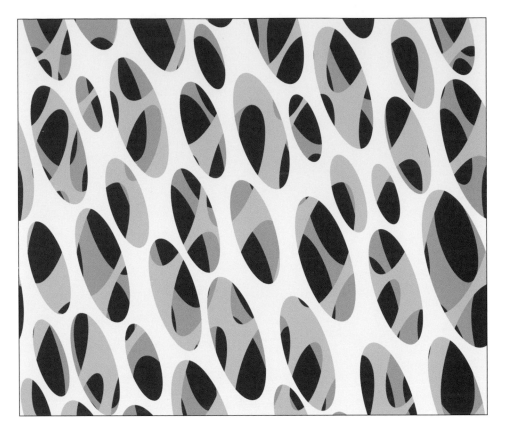

The midsole of a traditional running shoe is made of weblike foam polymers. As the shoe compresses, air is pushed into the holes between the polymers, making the foam "plump up" and cushion the foot. (Artist's representation.)

It's kind of like baking a cake. You stir up the batter and put it into the oven. As the batter is heated, the air molecules in the batter expand and the cake begins to rise. A similar thing happens in your running shoes—without the heat, of course. When the polymers in the foam are compressed, they release gas. The gas expands the space between the polymers, giving them room to flex.

But you don't want EVA polymers to flex too much or they'll eventually lose their shape. After enough impact, EVA foam stops bouncing back, and your shoes start to feel "flat" or "dead." So how do you make a running shoe that has flexibility and long-lasting support? That's where nanopolymers come in.

A nanopolymer consists of tiny chains of repeating nanoparticles.

Each nanopolymer is tiny—more than one thousand times smaller than a hair from your head. By inserting harder nanopolymers in between softer, more flexible nanopolymers, scientists can control how much the foam flexes.

Think of a kitchen sponge. When it's wet, you can bend it back and forth with ease. But what if you inserted a few straightened paper clips through the sponge? It would still bend, but the paper clips would give it more support. You wouldn't be able to wad the sponge up into a ball. The harder nanopolymers act like the paper clips. They restrict the softer nanopolymers from flexing too much and losing their shape.

Scientists believe the mix of hard and soft nanopolymers increases not only the foam's support and flexibility, but also its energy absorbance. The shoe lasts longer and is more durable.

Nanotubes add support to sprinting spikes

Sprinters use a special kind of running shoe called a spike, so named because metal spikes are attached to the front part of the bottom of the shoe. Sprinters are trained to run on the front of their feet and their toes. They use the spikes to dig into the porous material of the running track. This gives them better traction, or grip, and allows them to push off from the surface much harder, which increases their speed. Sprinting spikes do not have foam midsoles for cushion. Instead, the bottom of the shoe is typically composed of a hard type of plastic. In 2008 Adidas changed that.

Sprinters use special shoes called running spikes to grip the track surface and make it easier for them to push off.

After more than two years of research and development, engineers introduced a new type of running spike that was equipped with nanoplates.

A nanoplate is a strong piece of material reinforced with tightly bonded carbon nanotubes. The nanoplate fits along the bottom of the shoe, and spikes are attached to it. Since carbon nanotubes are so small, they create closer, much tighter bonds. This makes the nanoplate very strong and able to withstand lots of pounding.

The First Nanoplate Spike

The first company to use nanoplates in its shoes was Adidas. At the 2008 Beijing Olympics, US athlete Jeremy Wariner wore the Adidas Lone Star spikes in his four-hundred-meter run. The shoes were lighter and faster than regular spikes, and may very well have contributed to his silver-medal win.

Because carbon nanotubes are stronger than plastic, the nanoplate can be much thinner than a traditional plate—and about half its weight. The athlete has to expend less energy to lift the lighter spike off the ground, which leaves more energy for the important part—sprinting down the track!

Nanofibers are changing shoes inside and out

Shock absorbance, support, and light weight are all important—but what about comfort? You want your feet to feel good inside your running shoes. That's the job of the insole. The insole is the flexible pad that rests inside the shoe, on top of the foam midsole. The main job of the insole is to keep your foot comfortable and stable inside the shoe.

Many insoles are made of a special polyurethane foam created partially from recycled tires. The foam cushions your feet and has tiny openings that allow them to breathe. But sometimes these insoles can feel a little slippery.

A Japanese company called Teijin decided to fix that. Teijin engineers developed new insoles made of Nanofront, a high-strength nanofiber material that cradles the foot and keeps it in place. Each nanofiber is only 700 nanometers thick—more than one hundred times thinner than a human hair. The nanofibers are covered with tiny bumps, which increase their surface area and allow the material to grip the runner's foot better.

Although the nanofibers are tightly woven, there is still a tiny bit of space between them to absorb moisture, such as sweat. This keeps your feet dry and comfortable on long runs. Insoles made of Nanofront are also flexible and can bend and stretch with the shoe just like a regular insole.

Nanofibers are also being used by Nike to add support to the top of the shoe. Nanopolymers are spun together to form a nanofilament, a single nanofiber that is five times as strong as steel but still flexible. The filament is then woven through the material of the

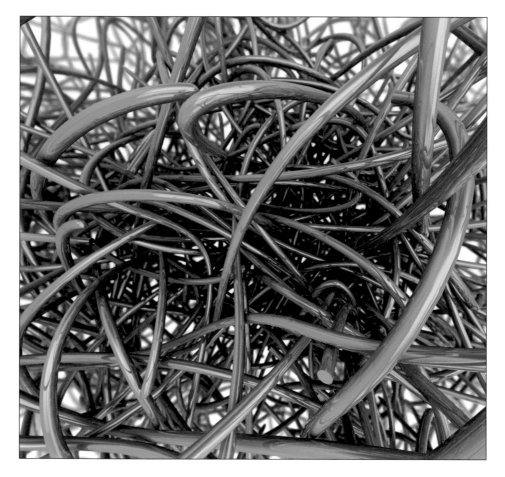

Nanofilaments spun from nanopolymers can be added to the top of a running shoe for improved comfort and support. (Artist's representation.)

Running shoes come in different sizes and shapes, and have different features—
just like runners themselves.

upper shoe to provide a comfortable, supportive frame for the foot.

Does using nanotechnology-enhanced shoes make you run faster? No one knows for sure. But if they cushion impact better, help you expend less energy, and make your feet more comfortable and stable, they might keep you running longer.

5
Super Science

Nanotechnology is found in almost every sport played today

Nanotechnology has made tennis rackets stronger and golf clubs more durable. It has made tennis balls and golf balls that fly faster and farther. It has even helped swimmers and runners break world records. But it doesn't stop there. Nanotech gear can be found in almost every sport played today.

Carbon nanotubes add strength but not weight to lacrosse and hockey sticks, as well as racing bikes. Using carbon nanotubes in a bicycle frame can reduce its weight by up to 20 percent. That means it will take less effort for a rider to cross the same distance or climb a steep hill.

Carbon nanofibers are being used in lacrosse sticks to give them added strength and durability.

A strong, lightweight bike is especially important in a race like the Tour de France, which is more than 2,000 miles (3,200 kilometers) long and includes many mountains.

Other kinds of carbon nanoparticles are being used to create lighter, faster snowboards. A nanocomposite applied to skis reduces friction, so the skier feels as if she is floating across the snow. Fabrics made with silver nanoparticles remove the stinky smell of sweat from athletes—and their socks. Pee-ew!

Stinky Socks No More!

Give a cheer! Your days of peeling off stinky, sweaty socks after a sports competition may soon be over. You can now get special socks made with nanosilver. The tiny fibers of silver are woven together with cotton and elastane (the elastic material found in spandex and Lycra) to provide a comfortable, stretchy fit—and one that is smell-free. How do these super socks defeat stinkiness? The silver nanofibers absorb the moisture produced by your feet and kill germs that cause odors. They can even improve blood supply and speed up healing of small cuts.

Nanotechnology is improving the safety of sports

Nanotechnology is also being used to solve one of the greatest problems in sports: safety. Concussions are a danger for athletes in many different sports. According to the Centers for Disease Control and Prevention (CDC), sports injuries cause up to 3.8 million concussions every year. A huge number of these concussions are suffered by football players, who experience hard hits as they tackle one another. To decrease the severity of concussions—and even prevent them—football manufacturers are using nanotechnology to develop a type of "smart" helmet.

The helmet contains a layer of foam that is in direct contact with a player's head. If the foam is compressed in a collision, nanoparticles in the foam give off low-voltage electricity. A sensor

Nanotechnology in football helmets is helping to protect players from concussions.

Concussions

Concussions don't happen to just football players. Lacrosse, hockey, and even soccer players can get concussions. A concussion occurs when you receive a direct or indirect blow to the head. Your brain bounces back and forth against the bones in your skull. This impact can cause headaches, dizziness, nausea, and other, more serious problems. The best thing for a concussion is rest. If you think you have a concussion, let your coach know right away—and see a doctor immediately.

in the helmet measures the voltage and sends a signal to a device that the coach holds in his hand. The device tells the coach that the player has had a hit to the head and how hard the hit was. The coach then can determine if the player needs to be sidelined for a few plays or taken out of the game entirely.

While the technology for this smart helmet is still being refined, a new nano-enhanced helmet is already countering concussions. Engineered by a company called Xenith, this helmet sports its own shock absorbers that rest on top of the player's head, inside the helmet. They act in the same way a car's shock absorbers do. When you go over a bump in a car, the shock absorbers cause the car to bounce up and down. They are like giant springs that absorb the dramatic change in movement, cushioning and protecting your body.

Likewise, when a football player is hit in the head, the shock absorbers inside the helmet compress slightly and then bounce back. They absorb most of the force from the blow, lessening the impact to the brain. The rubberlike elastomers that make up the shock absorbers are made with nanotechnology.

Every sport struggles with its own safety issues. Even a running track can be dangerous. The hard surface of a typical running

The surface of a nanotech track is bouncier, which is easier on runners' legs.

track causes pain for runners who train on it constantly. To improve track safety, engineers are adding nanopowders to make the surface bouncier, which in turn makes it easier on runners' legs.

Sports can be hard on the body. With nanotechnology, engineers hope to ease wear and tear—and prevent injury—for all athletes.

Nanotechnology is changing sports as we know it

Nanotechnology has dramatically changed competitive sports, quite possibly altering them forever. Athletes have firsthand access to groundbreaking engineering that boosts their performance to unprecedented levels. New personal records have been achieved, and new Olympic and world records have been set—all due to nanotechnology. But is it fair?

The data clearly show that nanotechnology can give an athlete an advantage. When Speedo's LZR Racer swimsuit was worn in the

Raphael Muñoz (Spain), Michael Phelps (USA), and Milorad Čavić (Serbia) celebrate their win at the FINA World Aquatics Championships in 2009. Full-body nanotech suits were still allowed at the time.

2008 Beijing Olympics, world records were broken in more than twenty-one of the thirty-four swimming events. Never before had so many swimming records been shattered in a single Olympics. So many people complained about the drastic change that in 2010 the

Is Nanotechnology Fair?

Does nanotechnology-enhanced equipment provide an unfair advantage? Maybe. Each sports organization is taking a look at how to regulate this new technology. But that may not be enough. What if a country can't afford the technology? Does that put it at a disadvantage? When the LZR Racer suits first came out, US swimmers were the only ones who had them. Then Japan got word of the suits and broke a bunch of sponsorship contracts to have their swimmers wear them, too. At the 2008 Olympics, the US and Japanese swimmers excelled. But countries that couldn't afford the suits didn't fare so well. Perhaps this is something that sports organizations should look at. What do you think?

Is Nanotechnology Safe?

As with any new tool, nanotechnology should be approached with an open mind and a cautious outlook. If you were to get a new bicycle with a lot of gadgets, you'd want to try it out a few times to make sure you could ride it safely. The same goes for nanotechnology. Nano-sized particles are not new and are found in nature. However, the way they are being manipulated to form new products is very new. Nanoparticles have unique properties that should be tested and understood. Since nanotechnology is becoming more and more widespread, it's in our best interest to keep studying it and its effects on us.

International Swimming Federation (FINA) outlawed the use of nanotech suits in competitions. Eventually, FINA lifted the ban, but it set strict regulations on the technology and restrictions on coverage. Men can wear suits that go from the waist to the knees only, and women are allowed coverage from the shoulders to the knees only.

Swimming is not the only sport to limit nanotechnology. Major League Baseball has banned the use of nanotech bats, and college players cannot use nanotech bats that function any better than standard wooden bats. Golf has strict guidelines for how clubs and balls can perform.

The term "technology doping" has been used to describe the effect technology is having on sports. Technology doping is when an athlete gains a competitive advantage from using equipment

SUPER FACT
Technology is always improving. Advances in bicycles, for example, have improved cyclists' performance by more than 221 percent in the last 111 years. Nanotechnology has just helped speed up the rate of improvement.

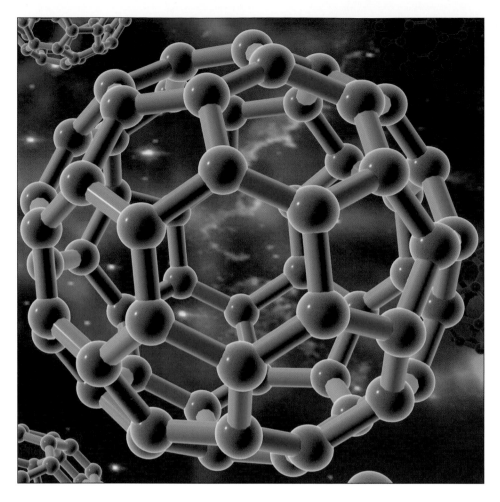

The future of nanotechnology in sports may include the buckyball, a spherical molecule made entirely of carbon atoms. (Artist's representation.)

enhanced with technology. Some people think that using nanotech equipment is similar to using drugs to boost performance. Others think that nanotech equipment is the wave of the future and should be accepted. It's a tricky line to walk—one that each sport's governing body needs to decide for itself. Will it allow technology that helps athletes break records and push the sport to new levels? Or will it decide that athletes need to train harder and compete based on their own athleticism? What do you think?

Nanotechnology Everywhere

Nanotechnology continues to expand not just in sports, but in all areas. Nanoparticles are being used in the fields of medicine and food production. They are helping to create new energy, clean up the environment, and even fight crime. In law enforcement, for example, nanotechnology is being used to identify fingerprints and biological matter from crime scenes. Nanotech engineers have also created fabric that is so slick and impenetrable that it can resist a knife thrust. This powerful and microscopic technology knows no bounds.

Nanotechnology is a new and exciting science

Nanotechnology promises a brave new world, full of constant invention that opens up amazing opportunities for all sports. Skis that fly faster down mountains. Kayaks that cut through water more quickly. Poles for vaulting higher into the air. World-record times will continue to drop. New records that seem impossible today will be set.

Regardless of all the enhancement nanotechnology offers, the focus of sports must remain on the athletes themselves. The athlete is the one who trains for hours a day—for weeks, months, or years—to achieve peak performance. All the super gear in the world cannot replace that. But it's still fascinating to see how nanotechnology is changing the face of sports—and to imagine where the tiniest of sciences may take us in the nano-world of tomorrow.

Author's Note

Why nanotechnology?

I have always loved science! In fact, at the age of seven, I started my own science club in my garage with a few kids in my neighborhood. We tracked bugs, looked at grass and plants under a microscope, and took things apart. We wanted to know how they worked. My love of science and engineering has grown with me over the years. It has changed the way I view the world. I love sports, too, and the Olympics are a huge deal in my house. So when I watched the 2008 Olympics and the controversy over the nanotech swimsuits arose, I was extremely interested. Technology and sports? To me, that is a fantastic—and intriguing—combination. I was hooked!

I began my research by educating myself about nanotechnology. I read books and magazines, and also reviewed many academic articles and journals from universities where nanotechnology topics are taught and researched. Here are just a few of those schools:

- Boston University: http://www.bu.edu/nano-bu
- Georgia Institute of Technology: http://www.ien.gatech.edu/
- Massachusetts Institute of Technology: http://newsoffice.mit.edu/topic/nanotech
- Northwestern University: http://www.iinano.org/

In addition, I accessed information from the many government agencies that work with nanotechnology on a daily basis:

- NASA: http://www.nasa.gov/centers/ames/research/technology-onepagers/nanotechnology-landing.html
- National Institutes of Health: http://public.csr.nih.gov/StudySections/IntegratedReviewGroups/BSTIRG/NANO/Pages/default.aspx
- National Nanotechnology Initiative: http://www.nano.gov/nanotech-101

Once I felt comfortable with my understanding of nanotechnology, I began investigating the sports angle. I did extensive research into all the products included in this book. However, some of the information is considered to be a company's intellectual property, or IP. That means the company protects the information very tightly so that other manufacturers cannot discover its secrets and copy its products. For the record, I did not have access to any IP from any company, but took all of my information from company websites and marketing literature.

Nanotechnology, like all new fields, is constantly changing. Scientists and engineers are always on the hunt for new ways to apply what they have learned. By the time you read this book, new super gear will have been developed. Some details about how nanotechnology is used in sports equipment will have changed. But the basic science will be the same.

This book would not have been possible without the people who helped me understand nanotechnology. For that I would like to thank my husband, Jon, a US Navy-trained nuclear engineer, now a consultant, and also Dr. Matthew Myntti, a PhD in materials-science engineering and president of Next Science, who agreed to be the expert reviewer for this book. Matt's knowledge of nanotechnology and its applications was immensely helpful. His dedication and attention to detail, too, were greatly appreciated. I would also like to thank Dr. Ben Topham, Assistant Professor of Chemistry at Longwood University, for his help in explaining a particularly tough chemistry concept. Finally, I would like to give a huge thank-you to my editor, Alyssa Mito Pusey, who stuck with me through the ins and outs of developing this complex—and often challenging—book.

Nanotechnology is a fascinating field that affects almost every aspect of your daily life. Take a look around you and see how many things you can discover that involve nanotechnology. I bet it's way more than you think!

 **Glossary**

atom: The basic building block of the universe.

bond: An attraction between two atoms or molecules that forms a connection to make a larger substance.

bottom-up manufacturing: Making a product by putting raw materials together.

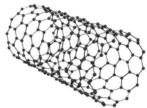

carbon nanotube: A form of carbon that is made by rolling a sheet of graphite into a cylinder. Carbon nanotubes are tiny, lightweight, and extremely strong.

composite: Made of different materials. A composite bat consists of carbon fibers combined with resin.

compression technology: A design that applies pressure to the body to form it into a specific shape. Competitive swimsuits use compression to make a swimmer's body more streamlined.

concussion: A blow to the head that can cause unconsciousness or injury to the brain.

deoxyribonucleic acid (DNA): The substance in your body that holds the code for every one of your cells.

drafting: A technique in which speed skaters skate close behind one another to reduce air resistance, or drag.

drag: Resistance of movement through a fluid such as water or air. Drag slows a moving object down.

elasticity: The ability to rebound, or bounce back. An aluminum baseball bat has high elasticity; when a ball hits the bat, the surface of the bat rebounds like a trampoline, reflecting energy back into the ball.

elastomer: An elastic polymer.

ethylene vinyl acetate (EVA): A rubberlike foam used in shoes and other products.

face: The part of a golf club that hits the ball.

friction: The resistance that an object encounters when it rubs against something else.

graphene: A form of carbon made by unrolling a carbon nanotube. Graphene is thought to be the strongest material in the world.

graphite: A form of carbon in which each carbon atom bonds weakly with three other carbon atoms. Graphite is soft and gray and found in pencils.

gravity: The force that attracts a body to the center of the Earth; the force of attraction between two objects.

grip: The part where you hold a golf club, tennis racket, or baseball bat.

head: The part of a golf club or tennis racket that is used to strike the ball.

insole: The inside part of a shoe that sits under the foot and on top of the midsole. It is sometimes removable.

lift: The height of an object as it flies through the air; the upward force that acts on a flying object.

mass: The amount of matter in an object.

midsole: A layer of material between the insole and the outer sole of a shoe. The midsole absorbs the shock of impact.

molecule: Two or more atoms that are bonded together.

nanocomposite: Made of different materials, including nanoparticles. A nanocomposite bat might consist of a combination of carbon nanotubes, carbon fibers, and resin.

nanofiber: A tiny fiber created at the nanoscale.

nanofilament: See *nanofiber*.

nanomanufacturing: The large-scale production of goods that incorporate nanotechnology.

nanomaterial: A material that is composed of nanoparticles.

nanometal: A metal consisting of nanoparticles.

nanometer: One-billionth of a meter.

nanoparticle: A microscopic particle less than one hundred nanometers in diameter.

nanoplate: A flat material made of nanoparticles. The nanoplate on the bottom of a sprinting spike consists of carbon nanotubes.

nanopolymer: A chain of repeating nanoparticles.

nanoscale: The level of measurement that deals with nanometers. Working "at the nanoscale" means working with particles measuring between one and one hundred nanometers in diameter.

nanotechnology: Science and engineering at the nanoscale, with particles that are less than one hundred nanometers in diameter.

outsole: The outer part of the bottom of a shoe. The outsole comes into contact with the ground.

point of impact: The place on an object where it collides with another object.

polymer: A large molecule that consists of repeating chains of smaller molecules.

polyurethane: A strong, flexible, man-made plastic that is used in foams, resins, and thousands of other materials.

reactive: Capable of bonding with other atoms, molecules, or nanoparticles.

reactivity: The tendency of one substance to react with another substance.

resin: A thick, sticky liquid that is used as a filler to provide strength in many products. Tree sap is a type of natural resin.

scanning tunneling microscope (STM): A microscope used to look at objects at the molecular level. An STM scans the surface of a nanoparticle and uses the information to create a three-dimensional image of the particle.

shaft: The long part of a golf club.

spandex: A man-made fiber known for its elasticity.

spike: A specialized running shoe with spikes on the bottom for better traction, or grip.

streamlined: Having a shape that allows movement through a fluid with very little resistance. A streamlined object can move quickly and easily through air or water.

surface area: The space that covers the outside of an object.

sweet spot: The best point of impact on a baseball bat, tennis racket, golf club, or other object. The sweet spot of a bat is the point where the majority of the batter's energy is transferred directly to the ball.

technology doping: When an athlete gains a competitive advantage from using equipment enhanced with technology.

top-down manufacturing: Making a product by eliminating excess material.

turbulence: Resistance to an object's movement through a fluid. Turbulence slows an object down and is characterized by bumpy movement or by curling streams of air or water behind the object.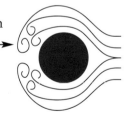

# Resources

Books

Buckley, James, Jr. *STEM in Sports: Technology.* Broomall, PA: Mason Crest, 2015.

Jefferis, David. *Micro Machines: Ultra-Small World of Nanotechnology.* New York: Crabtree, 2006.

Johnson, Rebecca L. *Nanotechnology.* Minneapolis, MN: Lerner Publications, 2006.

Ross, Stewart. *Sports Technology.* Mankato, MN: Smart Apple Media, 2012.

Websites

The websites listed below were current at the time of publication. To find out more about nanotechnology and sports, try searching for "nanotechnology and sports" with your favorite search engine.

Explain That Stuff!—Nanotechnology
This is a great resource for kids about the basics of nanotechnology and how it is used today.
http://www.explainthatstuff.com/nanotechnologyforkids.html

NanoKids
Developed by Rice University, this is a more structured program with workbooks, sample tests, and videos that go in-depth into nanotechnology for grades 3 and up. There are even teacher resources here!
http://www.nanokids.rice.edu/

Nanowerk
Take a peek inside many different aspects of nanotechnology application.
www.nanowerk.com/n_neatstuff.php

Nanozone
Set up by the Lawrence Hall of Science at the University of California, Berkeley, this interactive website has information, games, and videos about all things nanotech.
http://www.nanozone.org/

National Nanotechnology Infrastructure Network (NNIN)
For students in grades K–12, this site includes a nanotechnology magazine, ideas for science-fair projects, and lots of articles to satisfy your curiosity.
http://www.nnin.org/education-training/k-12-students

Source Notes

For bibliographic information about the sources mentioned in these notes, please see pages 68–69.

Page 22: Speed of great white shark: "Great White Shark," Smithsonian.

Page 22: ProTurboSpeed time savings: "Nike Unveils Track & Field Footwear and Apparel Innovations," Nike, Inc.

Page 22: Speed of Michael Phelps's butterfly swim: Santoso.

Page 22: "People would look at us . . . maybe it is.'" Stuart Isaac, quoted in "Record Breaking Benefits," NASA. Punctuation corrected.

Page 22: Effect of water flowing across swimmer's body: "Record Breaking Benefits," NASA.

Page 27: Drag reduction of nanotech swimsuit: Morrison.

Page 33: Speed of baseball hit with aluminum bat versus wooden bat: Berkow.

Page 33: Speed of MLB pitch: Sawchik.

Page 35: "It would take an elephant, . . . the thickness of Saran Wrap." James Hone, quoted in "Columbia Engineers Prove Graphene Is the Strongest Material," *Columbia News*.

Page 42: Usain Bolt's top speed: Dvorsky.

Page 42: Average human's top speed: "The Limits of Human Speed," National Council on Strength and Fitness.

Page 47: Thickness of Nanofront nanofiber: "Nanofibers Enhance Sports Shoes Performance," Nafigate.

Page 51: Weight reduction in carbon-nanotube bicycle frame: Kanellos.

Page 53: Number of sports-related concussions per year: "Facts for Physicians About Mild Traumatic Brain Injury (MTBI)," CDC.

Page 57: Improvement of cyclists' performance: Bardin.

Selected Bibliography

Bardin, Jon. "Is Technological Doping the Strongest Force in the Olympics?" *Los Angeles Times.* July 24, 2012. http://articles.latimes.com/2012/jul/24/science/la-sci-sn-is-technological-doping-the-strongest-force-in-the-olympics-20120724.

Berkow, Ira. "Metal Bats Are an Issue of Life and Death." *New York Times.* July 16, 2006. http://www.nytimes.com/2006/07/16/sports/baseball/16bats.html?pagewanted=all.

"Cerax Nanowax—Better Speed and Agility on the Slopes—New Product." AZoNano. Last modified June 11, 2013. http://www.azonano.com/article.aspx?ArticleID=615.

Columbia University. "Columbia Engineers Prove Graphene Is the Strongest Material." *Columbia News.* July 21, 2008. http://www.columbia.edu/cu/news/08/07/graphene.html.

D'Amato, Gary. "High-tech Suit Aims to Give U.S. Speedskaters Olympic Edge." *Milwaukee Journal Sentinel.* January 21, 2014. http://www.jsonline.com/sports/olympics/high-tech-mach-39-suit-aims-to-give-us-speedskaters-an-edge-b99188694z1-241406571.html.

Dusek, David. "Bridgestone 2014 Tour B330 Golf Balls." *Golfweek.* February 7, 2014. http://golfweek.com/news/2014/jan/21/bridgestone-2014-tour-b330-golf-balls/.

Dvorsky, George. "The Physics of Usain Bolt's World Record 100-Meter Dash." io9 blog. July 26, 2013. http://io9.com/the-physics-of-usain-bolts-world-record-100-meter-dash-924744818.

Evans, Jon. "Nanotech Clothing Fabric 'Never Gets Wet.'" *New Scientist.* November 24, 2008. https://www.newscientist.com/article/dn16126-nanotech-clothing-fabric-never-gets-wet/#.VYMqiyzbKpp.

"Facts for Physicians About Mild Traumatic Brain Injury (MTBI)." CDC. http://www.cdc.gov/headsup/pdfs/providers/facts_for_physicians_booklet-a.pdf.

"Great White Shark." Smithsonian National Museum of Natural History: Ocean Portal. Accessed August 19, 2015. http://ocean.si.edu/great-white-shark.

"i-EZONE: Driver Technology, Shaft Technology, Iron Technology." Yonex. Accessed July 10, 2015. http://www.yonex.com/i-ezone/technology/#iron.

"Interactive Molecules—Ice Structure." EDinformatics: The Interactive Library. 1999. http://www.edinformatics.com/interactive_molecules/ice.htm.

Johnson, Dexter. "Nanotechnology Offers Potential to Predict Football Concussions." IEEE Spectrum. November 7, 2013. http://spectrum.ieee.org/nanoclast/semiconductors/nanotechnology/nanotechnology-offers-fix-to-football-concussions.

Jones, Richard. "Nanotechnology and the Running Shoe." Engineering and Physical Sciences Research Council: The EPSRC Nanotechnology Image Library. 2005. http://www.nanofolio.org/images/gallery05/video1.php.

Kanellos, Michael. "Carbon Nanotubes Enter Tour de France." CNET. July 10, 2006.
http://www.cnet.com/news/carbon-nanotubes-enter-tour-de-france/.

"The Limits of Human Speed." National Council on Strength and Fitness. Accessed August 19, 2015. http://www.ncsf.org/enew/articles/articles-limitsofhumanspeed.aspx.

McArdle, Tamara. "Q & A: Why Do Tennis Balls Lose Their Bounce?" University of Illinois at Urbana-Champaign Department of Physics: Ask the Van. December 11, 2014.
https://van.physics.illinois.edu/qa/listing.php?id=951.

Morrison, Jim. "How Speedo Created a Record-Breaking Swimsuit." *Scientific American.*
July 27, 2012. http://www.scientificamerican.com/article/how-speedo-created-swimsuit/.

"Nanofibers Enhance Sports Shoes Performance," Nafigate: Nanofibers Gateway. July 12, 2002. http://www.nafigate.com/en/section/portal/app/news/detail/70066-nanofibers-enhance-sports-shoes-performance.

"Nike Unveils Track & Field Footwear and Apparel Innovations." Nike, Inc. February 21, 2012. http://news.nike.com/news/track-field-nike-pro-turbospeed-uniforms-and-nike-zoom-spikes.

Nosowitz, Dan. "Speedo's Super-Fast, Shark-Skin-Inspired Fastskin Swimsuit Is Actually Nothing Like a Shark's Skin." *Popular Science.* July 23, 2012.
http://www.popsci.com/technology/article/2012-07/speedos-super-fast-sharkskin-inspired-swimsuit-actually-nothing-sharks-skin.

"Physics of Baseball." American Physical Society: Physics Central. 2015.
http://www.physicscentral.com/explore/action/baseball.cfm.

"Record Breaking Benefits." NASA. October 31, 2012. https://www.nasa.gov/offices/oct/home/tech_record_breaking.html#.VUtoN_lVhBc.

Santoso, Alex. "Michael Phelps Vs. Goldfish: Who Is Faster?" Neatorama. August 18, 2008.
http://www.neatorama.com/2008/08/18/michael-phelps-vs-goldfish-who-is-faster/.

Sawchik, Travis. "MLB Pitchers Setting Velocity Records, Altering Balance of Power."
TribLIVE. March 29, 2014. http://triblive.com/sports/mlb/5423918-74/mph-velocity-cole#axzz3jBeBak18.

"Scanning Tunneling Microscope (STM)—How They Work and Their Applications."
AZoNano. Last modified June 11, 2013. http://www.azonano.com/article.aspx?ArticleID=1725.

"Technology: MA-1.0." Oncore Golf. 2015. http://www.oncoregolf.com/technology.

Wright, Chris. "Breakthroughs: 10 Technologies Changing the 2012 Olympics." Gear Patrol. July 26, 2012. http://gearpatrol.com/2012/07/26/10-technologies-changing-the-olympics/.

Zhao, Chao, Alparslan Oztekin, and Xuanhong Cheng. "Gravity-Induced Swirl of Nanoparticles in Microfluidics." *Journal of Nanoparticle Research.* April 21, 2013.
Accessed through Springer Link. http://link.springer.com/article/10.1007%2Fs11051-013-1611-8.

Image Credits

Front cover: Runner: Pete Saloutos/Shutterstock.com. Tennis player: bikeriderlondon/Shutterstock.com. Baseball player: Michael Mitchell/Shutterstock.com. Swimmer: BrunoRosa/Shutterstock.com. Background: Kateryna Kon/Shutterstock.com.

Title page: Central image: Peter Bernik/Shutterstock.com. Background: sakkmesterke/Shutterstock.com.

Page iv: Neale Cousland/Shutterstock.com.

Page vi: Limin Tong/Harvard University.

Page viii: cybrain/Shutterstock.com.

Page 2: Marvin Rich/Edinfomatics.com.

Page 3: Itub/Wikimedia Commons.

Page 4: 3drenderings/Shutterstock.com.

Page 5: xrender/Shutterstock.com.

Page 7: Left: Deep OV/Shutterstock.com. Right: Binh Thanh Bui/Shutterstock.com.

Page 10: Dmitry Kalinovsky/Shutterstock.com.

Page 11: xrender/Shutterstock.com.

Page 12: Frank Trixler, LMU/CeNS.

Page 13: Argonne National Laboratory.

Page 14: Mitch Gunn/Shutterstock.com.

Page 16: NASA.

Page 18: Paolo Bona/Shutterstock.com.

Page 19: Sophia M. Gholz, based on a NASA image.

Page 20: Paolo Bona/Shutterstock.com.

Page 23: Top: BoH/Wikimedia Commons. Bottom: Ike Li/Shutterstock.com.

Page 24: Pavel L Photo and Video/Shutterstock.com.

Page 25: Vinogradov Illya/Shutterstock.com.

Page 26: Hohenstein Laboratories, Germany.

Page 27: BrunoRosa/Shutterstock.com.

Page 28: Kevin Hill Illustration/Shutterstock.com.

Page 32: ogwen/Shutterstock.com.

Page 33: National Nanotechnology Coordination Office.

Page 34: Neale Cousland/Shutterstock.com.

Page 36: Inset: BONNINSTUDIO/Shutterstock.com. Background: Shilova Ekaterina/Shutterstock.com.

Page 37: Top: Chatchai Somwat/Shutterstock.com. Bottom: imagedb.com/Shutterstock.com.

Page 38: Sophia M. Gholz.

Page 39: David W. Leindecker/Shutterstock.com.

Page 40: Mikael Damkier/Shutterstock.com.

Page 42: Kaliva/Shutterstock.com.

Page 43: Sunny studio/Shutterstock.com.

Page 44: PGMart/Shutterstock.com.

Page 46: mezzotint/Shutterstock.com.

Page 48: Mmaxer/Shutterstock.com.

Page 49: Stefan Holm/Shutterstock.com.

Page 50: Aspen Photo/Shutterstock.com.

Page 52: Radu Razvan/Shutterstock.com.

Page 53: Richard Paul Kane/Shutterstock.com.

Page 55: bikeriderlondon/Shutterstock.com.

Page 56: Mitch Gunn/Shutterstock.com.

Page 58: Kateryna Kon/Shutterstock.com.

Page 62: Top: 3drenderings/Shutterstock.com. Bottom: ikayaki/Shutterstock.com.

Page 63: Top: Itub/Wikimedia Commons. Bottom: Jut/Shutterstock.com.

Page 64: Top: xrender/Shutterstock.com. Bottom: molekuul.be/Shutterstock.com.

Page 65: Top: Vaclav Volrab/Shutterstock.com. Bottom: BoH/Wikimedia Commons.

Back cover: Kateryna Kon/Shutterstock.com.

Decorative molecules: Carbon nanotubes on pages ii–iii, 20–21: 3drenderings/Shutterstock.com. Molecules on pages iii, v, 6, 13, 18–19, 26–27, 30–31, 34–35, 54–55, 59, 60, 61, 62, 66, 67, 68, 70, 71, 72: Jut/Shutterstock.com. Graphene on pages vii, 49, 67: Ekaterina/Shutterstock.com. DNA on page 45: ikayaki/Shutterstock.com.

Index

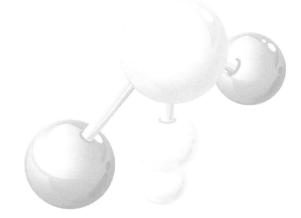